Student

Staying Wel

BY DR D(

C000095765

T ⵑ

Tania Richards Photography

Dr Dominique Thompson is a GP, young people's mental health expert, TEDx speaker, author and educator, with over 20 years of clinical experience caring for students, most recently as Director of Service at the University of Bristol Students' Health Service. It was for this work that she was named Bristol Healthcare Professional of the Year 2017.

She is a Clinical Advisor for the Royal College of GPs, and for Student Minds, the UK's student mental health charity. She was the GP member of the NICE Eating Disorders' guidelines development group, and the Universities UK StepChange and Minding Our Future committees. Dominique is also a member of the UK Mental Wellbeing in Higher Education group (MWBHE).

Dominique's TEDx talk, What I learnt from 78,000 GP consultations with university students, highlights some of the causes behind the recent rise in young people's mental health distress, and suggests ways in which everyone can better support the younger generation.

You can follow her on twitter @DrdomThompson and on Instagram as drdom99

First published in Great Britain 2019 by Trigger

The Foundation Centre
Navigation House, 48 Millgate, Newark
Nottinghamshire NG24 4TS UK

www.triggerpublishing.com

British Library Cataloguing in Publication Data

A CIP catalogue record for this book is available upon
request from the British Library

ISBN: 9781789560640

This book is also available in the following e-Book formats:

MOBI: 9781789560671
EPUB: 9781789560657

Cover design and typeset by Fusion Graphic Design Ltd

Printed and bound in Great Britain by Clays Ltd, Elcograf S.p.A

Paper from responsible sources

TRIGGER™
The mental health & wellbeing publisher

www.triggerpublishing.com

Thank you for purchasing this book.
You are making an incredible difference.

Proceeds from all Trigger books go directly to
The Shaw Mind Foundation, a global charity that focuses
entirely on mental health. To find out more about
The Shaw Mind Foundation, visit
www.shawmindfoundation.org

MISSION STATEMENT

Our goal is to make help and support available for every
single person in society, from all walks of life. We will
never stop offering hope. These are our promises.

Trigger and The Shaw Mind Foundation

the *Shaw* mind
FOUNDATION

Creating hope for children,
adults and families

For Jack.

ROLE DEFINITIONS

A Who's Who of Student Support

GP (general practitioner)

A GP is a medically qualified doctor who sees people in the community, not in a hospital. They are able to help with all conditions, although they may have a special interest, for example in skin problems or mental health. They are sometimes called "family doctors," and will often refer to specialists, such as psychiatrists or psychologists, for specific problems.

Counsellor

A counsellor offers a safe confidential space for individuals to talk. Counsellors help their clients explore their thoughts, feelings and actions to help them come to terms with life and find more hopeful and useful ways to approach their future. Counsellors will work in different ways depending on their training, but will always allow their client to take the lead in what they want to talk about. They do not offer advice, but through the empathic attention they give to their client's words, the client often discovers their own wisdom, helping them to lead a more fulfilling life.

Clinical Psychologist

A person who specialises in psychological or emotional conditions and mental health disorders. They will have specialised in the study of clinical psychology and will usually have a doctorate or PhD (though they're not medically qualified and will not able to prescribe medication). They assess people and diagnose mental health conditions or problems. They are trained in using talking and behavioural interventions specifically tailored to treat psychological disorders. They may use a range of therapy approaches which vary from psychodynamic to cognitive behavioural therapy and family and couples' therapies, to interpersonal approaches. They base their assessment and treatment methods on scientific principles and outcomes, and will use the best evidenced method that helps to treat an individual.

Therapist

A term for professionals who use talking and behavioural therapies to support people with mental health conditions.

Psychiatrist

A medically qualified doctor who specialises in mental health conditions (also called psychiatric conditions) who can assess, make a diagnosis, offer advice, and prescribe medications. A psychiatrist is the only person who can prescribe some specialist medications. They work with GPs, therapists, psychologists and counsellors, and will usually recommend a type of talking or behavioural treatment.

CONTENTS

INTRODUCTION

Many students, when asked, say they wish they had been better prepared for university and had been given a more realistic idea of what to expect and how to look after themselves once there.

So here it is, a short book that intends to do just that.

This book will help you prepare for the move to uni life (even if you will still be living at home, you will likely be moving to a different way of life) and prepare for some of the pressures and challenges that come with being a student.

Timeline

The book will follow the timeline of a new student's experiences, starting with preparation for uni, moving onto Welcome Week (previously known as Freshers' Week). It will then wind its way through the first, second, and third terms, taking into consideration the effect holidays can have. Finally, there will be a specific section on exams and assignments, which can cause particular stress. This will help you find the bits most relevant to you at different times of the year.

Throughout the book you will read comments and quotes from students and recent graduates about what they discovered, or wish they had known, about starting life at uni and looking after themselves.

Useful resources, websites, apps, and further info will be found at relevant points along the way.

CHAPTER 1

PREPARING FOR UNI

> 'I would have felt better prepared if there was not such an expectation for uni to be the best part of your life.'

This quote, from a student who took part in a survey in 2018, sums up the feelings of so many students. It's often said that university years are the best years of your life, but it's fair to say that – while it's hoped that your uni years are a positive experience – they are *rarely* the best of anyone's life! They involve significant hard work, they are tiring, and they are *often* a lot of fun. But not always.

It's important to have a more realistic view of these years. They are a path to useful qualifications and they give you an opportunity to try new things, meet new people, be yourself, and discover independence. But they are also academically challenging, exhausting, financially strained, testing of your patience (often with friends, flatmates, and relationships), and highly pressured. You need to step onto that path ready for highs and lows, and also ready to bounce back when the going gets tough.

Here's another quote from that survey:

'It's okay to have ups and downs at uni. Having downs doesn't mean you've failed.'

TOP TIP ADDRESSING PRE-UNI WORRIES

If you have specific worries about going to uni, sit down with a trusted friend or family member and make a list of them. Then work through them and address those worries together. It may help to put the different worries into categories, such as "money", "socialising", or "living away from home", and then make an action plan for each one (Thompson and Cole-King, 2018). For more top tips like these, see the lists at the end of the book.

What Do Teachers Think?

'Sixth formers are too *focused* on short term grades and academic results and *unable* to *visualise* life at uni.'

This was the conclusion of a study of UK teachers in 2017, who were worried about their pupils being unprepared for uni life but were keen to help them get ready (Hughes, Massey, Williams, 2017).

Does that sound like you when you were in the Sixth Form? Were you almost entirely focused on the next week's grades or exam results, and just assuming that life at uni would work itself out?

Hopefully this book will help you to think ahead, *visualise* what life might be like, consider potential problems, and plan your response in advance. This will better equip you to ride the waves of those testing but exciting times ahead.

Let's start with health issues.

Health Issues and Avoiding "Magical Thinking"

Doctors in university health centres get pretty used to seeing students who arrive at uni with the hope that their medical issues, particularly mental health issues, will somehow go away as they start their new lives.

It is very common for students to long for this (somewhat miraculous) situation. That their issues should suddenly fade into the background – the anxiety that plagued their A Levels, the obsessive-compulsive behaviours that made them late for everything, the eating issues that ruined their social lives before uni – is a wonderful and understandable thing to wish for. But sadly, it rarely (if ever) happens.

This means that doctors regularly see a significant number of students who find themselves, about four or six weeks into term, struggling with their new life and academic pressures. They may also be desperate for help as their previous issues, which they have tried to ignore or move on from, rear their ugly heads once more.

In a few cases, the symptoms become bad enough to cause the students to suspend studies (take a "leave of absence") soon after arrival. This is a real shame for them as, with a little planning in advance and co-ordination of healthcare, the need to put their studies on hold so soon could perhaps be avoided.

So let's be really clear at this point, so that you can start uni life as you mean to go on ... *feeling and functioning well*.

If you had mental health or emotional issues *before* starting uni, certainly in the two or three years immediately prior, then you are very likely to have similar or related issues *after* starting or when your stress levels rise. So it is better to discuss this in advance, continue any medication and therapy, and *not suddenly stop treatment and support*. It does not have to stop you having a good and successful time. Dealing with the issues up front is going to help; ignoring them is likely to make things worse. We want to avoid this situation.

From yet another student in my survey:

'I knew I'd need help before I arrived, but I left it far too late. Now I'm still on the waiting list for treatment.'

Pre-Uni Health Checklist

1. Book an appointment with your usual GP at home before heading off to uni, to discuss your health issues. Arrange a letter to take (they can provide a printout of your health record summary) in case there is a delay in health records switching between home and university doctors, and ask for an appropriate supply of medication (two months is usual) so that you don't run out.

2. If you are under the care of a specialist doctor, ask them to refer you to the specialist team in your new uni location or discuss with them when you will see them for follow-up in the holidays. Again a summary letter can be helpful to take with you (emailed to you so you can forward it to the new doctor). If you are currently in active psychological treatment, you will need to find an appropriate professional to continue your CBT, or a psychologist. Alternatively, you may be able to continue with your current therapist via Skype, or book in sessions during term breaks. You may also be able to have some sessions which aim to prepare you for your uni life.

3. If you receive medications, medical devices, or equipment that may be difficult to obtain in your

new uni town, plan ahead so that you have plenty of supplies and know how to get the next quantity. For example, GPs cannot prescribe some medications for ADHD (Attention Deficit Hyperactivity Disorder) and they can only be prescribed by specialist doctors, so problems can arise when a student runs out and has to go without, because their uni GP can't prescribe them. This is also an issue for international students arriving in a country where their medications do not exist or are not licensed. This can include contraceptive pills, psychiatric medication, and allergy medications. Plan ahead!

4. Before arriving at your new uni, check out their website "health and wellbeing" section (sometimes called "student support") to see what they recommend for support relevant to your health issues. Connect with the disability team if you have known physical or mental health problems, to see if you are eligible for financial or practical help (government money is sometimes available). Talk to your uni wellbeing teams in advance of arrival.

5. On arrival in your new uni "home", register with a local GP. This may mean filling in your details online or completing a paper form for the practice. The uni may have a health team on campus, or they may recommend a local GP surgery with whom they have links. Ask other students which GPs they recommend. If the practice is not a student specific one, ask the receptionist if any of the GPs have a particular interest in student or young adult health, or in

the health condition that you have (for example diabetes or ulcerative colitis).

6. Try to make the call to book an appointment with the GP or register with them yourself. If you are anxious about this, ask a trusted person to sit next to you as you make the call. They could even go with you to your first appointment.

7. Take a small first-aid kit with you to uni. Put in some plasters, pain killers, dressings and paper tape, paper stitches, and so on, and make sure you know how to use or take them! Be prepared! If you're sexually active you should also take condoms with you.

8. If you are not used to getting prescriptions or buying over-the-counter medications such as for flu, colds, or allergies, then familiarise yourself with the basics, wander round a pharmacy, and ask friends or family how the prescription process works.

9. If you're not familiar with the NHS in general, read a bit about it on the main website (nhs.uk), or read a leaflet for international students on how it all works. This one is on the website of the University of Bristol Students' Health Service http://www.bristol.ac.uk/students-health/international-students/

10. Check which immunisations (vaccines) are recommended before arrival at uni, for example against mumps, measles, rubella, or meningitis. Get yourself immunised before you move in with several hundred students from all over the world, who may be unwitting carriers of

infection, and differently immune to you!
Take a copy of all your immunisations
with you to uni.

11. Have a dental and eye test before you leave
home. Once you're in the swing of things you
won't want to worry about eyes and teeth, and it
may prevent issues arising when you're living a
busy student life.

In Summary

Preparation is key to ensuring as smooth a start to uni life as possible. There are loads of things you can do to prepare in advance of arrival – some of which you may never have considered before, or which may seem obvious or common sense – but often, in the excitement and rush of heading off, they can be forgotten. Some, such as vaccinations, can even be potentially lifesaving.

So make a list, check it through with trusted friends and family, and get yourself ready for transition to your new life!

CHAPTER 2

LIFE AND DAILY LIVING SKILLS

So now that you've got your healthcare sorted (and if you don't look after your health, you're unlikely to be able to enjoy the rest of your uni experience as much as you might), let's think about other things you might need to think about to prepare for your new adventure.

Cookery 101

People who work in universities often say they are amazed at how few secondary school pupils or new uni students can cook. Yet it is a basic survival skill. The story of the newly arrived student who blew up the hall of residence's kitchen on day one, having tried to microwave a *whole* tin of beans (yes, including the tin!) is a perfect illustration of what can happen when someone with no idea what they're doing suddenly has to "cook".

A simple plan here might be to learn three or four of your favourite, but basic, tasty dishes from scratch (for example, spaghetti Bolognese, cottage pie, baked fish, or veggie lasagne) before you come to uni or when you know you are going to need to cook for yourself and flatmates. Then you can rely on these to get you through the first few opportunities to cook while learning a few more from other people, TV programmes, blogs, or recipe books along the way.

A great piece of advice to keep you reasonably healthy if you *do* have to rely on some convenience foods is to try to make a meal every few days that "doesn't have any labels" – in other words, using fresh or individual ingredients rather than ready meals or takeaways.

Laundry

Another story from week one at uni is from a student who watched as a fellow first year emptied half a box of laundry powder into the machine she was using to wash her clothes. It was clear the student had never done her own washing before and had no idea how much powder to use (a small cupful, in case you're interested!). Comedy bubbles and frothing from the machine ensued, but it wasn't a great start to independent life!

Simply being familiar with washing machines, laundrettes, or the basics of washing and ironing can be really useful once you are on your own and having to look after your clothes. Clearly many young people have done their own laundry from a young age, but not all, so this is a quick nudge to think about it!

Financial Skills

You don't need to be a money expert to know that money can have a significant impact on people's health and wellbeing. So it is important to have a basic idea about how to budget sensibly at uni from day one, and it's definitely worth considering how you might earn some extra money while at uni or during the holidays. Clearly, with some full-time courses it is not possible to study, rest, *and* have a job, but a bit of bar work, restaurant work, babysitting, or dog walking for uni staff may help earn a little cash. And holiday jobs are definitely possible.

For expert budget advice it is worth looking at dedicated websites and reading articles written by experts. There are some examples in the resources at the end of this book.

Being money smart may not sound cool, but you will definitely feel less stressed (and a tiny bit smug!).

Becoming Independent

You may only be reading this book as you arrive at uni, but if you have a chance to think about this one prior to arrival then this is the time to get yourself ready to be independent from your parents.

The last year or two before leaving home is a good time to start to prepare for uni life. One example is to use public transport or a bike to get around, rather than expecting your folks to drive you everywhere. Even if they offer, it's okay to say 'No thank you' and tell them you'll catch the bus, walk, or cycle when it's safe to do so. If you have the opportunity to learn to drive, it's worth doing it even if you don't have your own car for a while. It's a great skill to have and it's considered by many employers to be an essential skill. It will make you feel independent, and pretty impressed with yourself for getting on and doing it.

Open Days

Although it's now common for parents to go along to open days, consider going on your own. It's your life and where you go and what you study is your choice. There may be situations which require you to involve parents or carers – or you may simply want to involve them anyway – but ensure that the decisions you take are yours.

Arrivals Day

Once you do arrive at uni on the first day of term, encourage family to drop you off but not to hang around with you for too long. Perhaps encourage them to go for a cup of tea, have a walk around, or visit the campus without you. But they should let you get on with things, meet people, do your own first shop or make your bed yourself, as that is an important way to establish your new independence. Encourage your parents not to stay and use any "parent accommodation" that might be provided by the halls of residence, unless they have an exhausting journey requiring a stopover.

A good tip from another student, to ease the initial introductions to new flatmates, is 'Take games or biscuits; something you can share with other people and socialise with.'

Another great tip is not to go home for the first four weeks of university, otherwise you will miss out on loads of early bonding time, parties, sitting chatting in people's rooms or lounges, early events with clubs and societies, and so on. You might feel a bit down or lonely but try to rally and push through and chat with people. Speak to family and friends at home but try to stay on campus so that you feel part of your new community.

Contacting Home

It's entirely normal to want to stay in touch with family and friends from home once you arrive at uni, but it may be worth discussing the frequency of such contact before you leave, especially with parents or carers, as they may have an expectation of how often you will check in, which might differ from yours. This avoids misunderstanding and the possibility of them calling the police when you don't text or WhatsApp them every 24 hours because you're sleeping off the effects of Welcome Week or possibly with a new found "friend" from the night before. (The police scenario has definitely happened!)

Agreeing frequency of contact (and which format that will take – will it be text, call, Messenger, Facebook?) is key here, so be clear. It's best *not* to agree to contact every 24 hours or more often anyway, as this allows for unexpected changes in timetables, activities, trips, and sleep patterns and so on.

Something along the lines of *a message every other day*, and a call once or twice a week might be a good balance. It's up to you, but plan it in advance to avoid parental stress and calls to the authorities when you are late checking in.

In Summary

Some of these life or "independent living" skills may be things you have been doing for years, and others may be completely new to you, but they can make all the difference to settling in and staying on top of things at uni. Once academic work starts and the deadlines become real, you will be super focused on those and on going out and enjoying your new social life, so you won't want to be worrying about food or laundry! Make sure you are in charge of your money, social, and transport needs, so that you can relax and have a good time.

CHAPTER 3

WELCOME WEEK

This is a big week.

Welcome Week has assumed almost legendary and somewhat overwhelming status over the decades, which can feel like a huge pressure for new students. Not only are you *supposed* to be making "friends for life" and starting a course that could "transform your future", but you're expected to have the *best time ever* with loads of people you don't know, in a new place, while being the best version of yourself. It's exhausting!

So let's see what the reality is really like and what recent students have said about Welcome Week, or "Freshers" as it is often called. It may help to put things into perspective.

What Happens in Welcome Week?

You will be hit with a whole lot of new information.

TOP TIPS

- Make a note of the important things, such as where your room is, where you eat, where you need to register for your course, where you need to register for healthcare, and where the student advice or support centre is.
- Add important new uni contacts to your phone and get a sense of the bus routes or cycle paths.

- Walk around the relevant bits of campus or areas of the uni so that you become familiar with them before lectures start.
- Find out where to do laundry and where the residence / accommodation staff can be found if needed (where to enquire about security, new lightbulbs, or to sort broken furniture etc.).
- Go along to welcome meetings, as a lot of useful info is given out in one place.
- If you haven't had all your relevant immunisations (meningitis or MMR vaccines and so on) by now, then they will be available somewhere nearby, like at the local GP practice, so go along and have them. It may literally save your life.
- Register with the GP when you're there too, if you haven't already done this.
- Check where the counselling and support services are, even if you don't need them. You or your friends might at some point.

The *sensory overload* that is common in Welcome Week can be particularly overwhelming for some students who are sensitive to this, such as those with Asperger's disorder (a type of Autism Spectrum disorder) or social anxiety, so don't worry if this is you. Just take it slowly, sit quietly at the back, listen, and take it all in, in your own time and at your own pace. Then have breaks if you need them but try not to avoid everything or you will miss out.

And one of the best bits of student advice for everyone …

'It is okay to say no to things and that you need time to yourself as well.'

Welcome (or Fresher's) Fair

This is one tradition worth checking out: the opportunity to see all the clubs, societies, and organisations that the

Students' Union offers, alongside entertainment / gigs and a chance to find out what your new home is all about.

Advice from some students includes 'Join clubs and societies – they're full of like-minded people and making friends there is easier than on your course' and 'To meet new people initially you may have to try things that you might not end up enjoying, for example joining the frisbee club!'

Resist the temptation to sign up for everything but take care not to go the other way and only join groups that are good for your CV. Give the "fun" clubs like "ChocolateSoc" or knitting societies a chance too.

Most people do have periods of feeling lonely, and it is important to get involved with societies and non-academic interests early on. Uni is a fantastic opportunity to meet people and try new things – it's not just an academic tick box; it's also a whole new world of opportunity! You might discover you have a natural talent for Quidditch, Ultimate Frisbee, journalism, or another activity you have never tried. You might even have a passion for cheese (yes there are CheeseSoc groups!) or barbershop singing.

Maybe approach the fair with the plan to join one activity you know you will like and have tried before, and one thing you have never tried, or always wanted to … just don't spend all your money joining clubs, on day one of uni!

Take time out if needed. Don't forget that if it's all getting a bit much, you can have a break and sit quietly in your room to have some time alone. Or you could sit with a few friends or new flatmates and just chat, eat some snacks, and get to know each other.

Initiation Rites and Ceremonies

Most UK universities have outlawed these ceremonies, which were usually related to sports clubs or specific courses. However, it is fair to assume that many may have gone "underground" and you may still be invited to take part or witness them. The strong message here is steer clear (or fake an illness, allergy, or medical condition)!

Unless they are a gentle introduction to the rest of the team or your course-mates (which is not likely!) then they usually involve significant amounts of alcohol and regrettable, if not highly unsanitary, behaviour. For example, there have been cases that have involved crawling though disgusting muck to get to a pint of beer at the end – resulting in terrible tummy upsets in the new students and so on.

Peer pressure can be a terrible thing, but it's just fine to take a deep breath, say no thanks, and walk away. You won't be the only one who feels like that, and hopefully you won't be the only one to make your voice heard.

In the most serious cases that you may have read about in the media, students have died as a consequence of excessive alcohol or mixing different alcohols in large volumes. They have even drowned on their way home by falling into local rivers and canals. Initiation ceremonies rarely end well. Bear this in mind when making up your mind about whether or not to get involved.

Clubbing

> 'There's nothing wrong with not wanting to go out clubbing all the time, and many people also feel this way.'

This is one of the most obvious pressures of Freshers', or Welcome Week, with club nights and special events competing for your attention. You don't have to say yes to everything. Again, the key here is moderation.

Pick a couple of events that really appeal and go with some new people as an opportunity to get to know them. See whether they share your sense of what a good time is and whether they share your taste in music. Go home when you want to; don't feel you have to stay if you're not having fun. Clubbing isn't for everyone; there are other ways of making friends.

New Friends and Relationships

One of the best bits of advice from the student survey was this: 'Don't get pulled into intense relationships early on. You might not even meet your long-term friends until after Christmas.' In other words, don't make "panic friends"!

Others advised, 'Take breaks and be patient. Be patient with finding your "place" at uni and with finding friends. It's better to wait for those genuine and good friendships rather than panicking and forming and holding on to friendships that shouldn't be there. There are so many people at university and you don't have to change anything about yourself to fit in with people who aren't really a good fit. Wait for those you just click with.'

Be friendly, sure, but don't feel you have to be best friends with everyone you meet. Who knows who your "forever friends" will be, or even if you will stay in touch with any of these people once you leave uni. Some people form strong friendships at uni; others form relaxed relationships but make much closer friends in their place of work, or when they travel, join a sports club, or have children later in life, for example.

As one student said, 'Do not give in to the fear of missing out simply to be part of the crowd. You will eventually find people you get along with by being true to yourself.'

Take your time to get to know lots of people, don't allow your social circle to be too narrow, and say yes to new offers to meet up and go out, as long as you feel comfortable with that person. And if anyone acts "off" towards you because you are making other new friends and not just spending time with them, be very careful as they may be overly demanding and "needy" of you.

This goes for new romantic relationships too.

Romance

Falling in Fresher love …

It is common to fall in love in Welcome Week! The sheer number of cute new people to meet is impressive, and an easy trap to fall into is a co-dependent relationship with your new partner, where you become inseparable while everyone else is making lots of new friends. This may cause problems for you later, if or when the new relationship breaks down, as they often do. You will be left with few friends to support you when everyone else has connected and settled into new social groups.

So take your time. Meet and maybe date people but don't get too committed too quickly, either to new friends or boy / girlfriends.

And remember, there will be downs as well as ups at the beginning. We will talk more about loneliness later on in the book. Be prepared that you will, from time to time, feel sad and lonely. This will pass.

Alcohol

When students were asked what they had to say about drinking and alcohol in Welcome Week (and beyond!) there were two sides to their responses.

'Be prepared for the drinking culture,' one student suggested. Another said, 'It would have been useful to dispel the myths about drink and drugs that a lot of people like to think is normal for Freshers' Week.'

In other words, there is clearly an emphasis on drinking at uni and this culture can be quite forceful during Welcome Week in particular, but it may not be as bad as you expect. If it is there, you may be able to avoid it – or handle it – better than you think.

The fact of the matter is that young people simply don't drink as much alcohol as previous generations did. In fact, according to the National Union of Students' survey in 2018, about 1 in 5 students is now teetotal (doesn't drink alcohol at all). This fits with the overall rise in teetotal 16–24-year-old young adults in the UK, with 1 in 4 no longer drinking alcohol at all (John, 2017). Universities are recognising this trend and have responded by providing alcohol-free halls of residence in many UK cities. You might want to consider this, whether or not you drink, to ensure a calmer, quieter place to live and study, perhaps?

So, as you arrive at uni, you may find it possible to be careful with your alcohol intake – or choose not to drink – with less peer pressure than you expected and with more students choosing to be moderate like you.

Don't be afraid to be yourself and say when you've had enough or say "No thanks" if you don't want any at all. Or as one student put it, 'Don't drink. Don't go anywhere near drugs.'

And if you are going to drink, then this is a great piece of advice too!

'If you're going to be drinking a lot, then make sure you're balancing that with looking after your physical health in other ways, such as sleeping, exercising, and eating well.'

If you *are* going to drink, try to spread your intake over the week rather than having a lot on one or two evenings a week (binge drinking). You may like to space your drinking evenings and not drink every night. You can try spacing your drinks, having a non-alcoholic one between alcoholic drinks. Pace yourself and try to really reduce your drinking around exam times, as it can interfere with revision, learning and sleep, all of which are crucial for academic success.

Sex: A Word About Condoms ...

The latest generation of students and young adults has been really impressive in reducing their use of alcohol, cigarettes, and drugs. They have also significantly reduced unplanned pregnancies, which is great. What hasn't been so reassuring is the rising number of certain sexually transmitted infections (STIs).

Every autumn term, uni GPs unfortunately see quite a lot of young people a few weeks after Welcome Week who have got carried away in the excitement of "meeting" new people and who need to be tested for sexual infections. Other times they are subsequently contacted by someone they "met" in Welcome Week advising them to get treatment too, as that person has now been diagnosed with an STI!

So it seems that, while people *are* thinking about safe sex in terms of not getting pregnant and relying on pills, injections, coils, and implants to achieve this, condoms *aren't* getting such a look-in. The consequence is rising numbers of gonorrhoea and syphilis infections (Waters, 2018), which is bad news for your generation's fertility. It also causes unpleasant symptoms (and some other potentially long-term complications).

According to Public Health England, the most at-risk groups for STIs are heterosexual 15–24-year-olds, black or ethnic minorities, and gay, bisexual, or other men who have sex with men. So please *use condoms*!

There has also been a big decrease in screening for chlamydia (Public Health England reports), which may be related to reduced government funding of testing. But there are many places to get tested, most of them for free, so GPs (and Public Health England) strongly recommend an *annual check-up* like a car MOT, for all STIs! Search online or ask at a pharmacy to find local free testing for STIs in your area. Some will offer postal kits too, which is even easier. Or ask the nurses at your GP practice for advice.

And remember ...

In Summary

> 'It's important to know that if you don't like Freshers' Week, then that doesn't make you weird or mean there's something wrong with you. It doesn't mean that you're not cut out for uni. It's so normal — you're in a new place, doing a new subject, forced into new friendships with people you may or may not like at all ... it takes time to settle in, but the perception is that you're supposed to have the most amazing time from day one.'

Freshers week can be great fun, but it can be hectic and tiring, so try to pace yourself and listen to your instincts. There will be a lot to take in, loads of new information, the temptation to join millions of societies, and say 'Yes' to everything. Don't feel you have to be friends with everyone, exert some self-control when you need or want to around drink, drugs, and sex, and make sure you look after yourself in what can be an exhausting and overwhelming few days! It may not be the best week at uni but it can be memorable!

CHAPTER 4

TERM ONE: FINDING YOUR FEET

Let's hear from some of those students again, this time on the subject of balancing academic work with social activities ...

Getting into Your Studies

'Go to every single lecture; it feels worse if you stay in all day doing nothing and the stress of missing out on new material piles up fast.'

'Don't do too much, but also don't allow yourself to be isolated – go to events and meet people. Do your uni work but then find something you enjoy for yourself.'

Starting life at uni means many things, but importantly, of course, it means learning a new subject or developing a deeper knowledge of a favourite area. This will likely involve discovering new *ways* to learn, as well as adapting to a different level of flexibility and freedom to study when and how you like.

Although class attendance is, in many places, loosely monitored at uni, this is not like school or having a job, where if you don't show up various measures will be put in place. In those circumstances, people will spring into action to find you and find out what's going on. But at uni, tech allows you to study from your room, catch up later online, and also, of course, link up with people from your course to catch up on lost work.

There are obvious pros and cons to all of this freedom and autonomy, but what the students quoted here are stating, from their own experiences, is to try to keep up as you go along for your own sake, to keep your stress to a minimum. But, if you *do* need a day off to recover or rest then take it, because presenteeism (turning up when you're ill and should be at home) is bad for you too.

It can take time to adapt to the new pace of work. You might be given a term to write an essay, for example, or a year to do a project and write it up (and often in groups), and this is where you will need to try to see what works for you.

It's best not to leave everything until the last minute, of course, but it is proven to be better to work on longer-term projects gradually, coming back to them a few times, allowing ideas to percolate through your brain where possible, rather than trying to sit down and write it all at once. The evidence for this and more, if you're interested in knowing about effective and efficient ways that we learn, is in an excellent book by Benedict Carey called *How We Learn*. It is well worth a look!

Group Work

Working in groups brings its own stresses, and students commonly say that this is one of the skills that they struggle with most because of the need to adapt to other people's approaches to work, deadlines, and responsibility. Do the others take a fair share of the work? Are they control freaks, or do you not see them from one week to the next? These are all common scenarios in group work.

Many universities offer study skills classes and opportunities to discuss such challenges, so it might well be worth asking your academic tutor or support staff about these. There are also some excellent books for students that address this; see the resources page for suggestions.

Finding Your "Tribe"

In and among the work, of course, is the opportunity to meet new people from all over the world, and with whom you might form deep and long-lasting friendships over shared political or social views. Maybe at school you always felt like the odd one out, but at uni many people find that they finally connect with others like them. They meet their "tribe" and it can be very fulfilling and affirming to feel connected to others in this way.

Take your time to chat to lots of different people, and perhaps take up opportunities to socialise through your course as well as in the more traditional ways, to maximise your opportunities to meet people.

'Try lots of things – from societies to course lunches. Go out and meet as many people as possible in the first few weeks, then you can choose who to stick with.'

Loneliness

Of course, it's also true that it can seem very difficult to meet new people or make friends in this huge new environment, with so many strangers and too many opportunities to choose from.

'The hardest things were not immediately having a stable group of friends to rely on and sometimes being in unavoidable but uncomfortable situations, as well as feelings of loneliness and sometimes isolation, especially to start with.'

All these questions and more flood through your brain.

'Stay in close contact with your friends at home, but also reach out to make friends in university.'

It can seem like the easiest thing in the world to retreat to your room, go online, chat to friends and family on your phone, and ignore the new and seemingly "scary" outside world. But this is not a great option. If at all possible, I would suggest you try to venture out. Start by walking around, smile at people who seem friendly in safe places like the lecture theatre or hall / residential shared spaces. Then maybe build up to starting a conversation about something you will likely have in common, like the lecturer or your course.

And don't forget to exercise and get out and about. Make sure you explore your new home area.

TOP TIPS

Good Conversation Starters

- 'What do you think of the course so far?'
- 'Where did you live before uni?'
- 'That lecturer seems nice; have you heard much about them?'
- 'What do you think of the food here?'
- 'Have you joined any of the teams or societies yet?'

And so on. These are gentle opening questions that allow you to see how someone will respond, whether they smile, and whether they are chatty or anxious or grumpy. And just like that, you will have pushed back against becoming isolated and lonely (without even asking what they did at A Level!).

International Students

For international students there can be particular hurdles involved with arriving in a new country, experiencing a new culture and a different time zone to your family and friends, and managing all of this in a new language while trying to study a difficult academic subject.

I have known of students staying up every night to video call home at 3.00 am, as that is the only time their families can speak. I've also known of students dealing with civil war back home. Both are very different scenarios but both can cause real alienation from the other students, who are not having to cope with such difficulties or trauma.

There are usually excellent services and support options available for international students, provided by staff teams or the Students' Union. They can help you to feel less isolated and alone and they are ready to help with everything from visa issues to day trips, academic challenges, or health concerns. Look for the International Student Office or team.

There are also increasing numbers of websites and resources specialising in international student support. It can help to link up with other overseas students through societies and the Students' Union or international organisations in the city or town you live in. You are not alone!

Students with Communication or Social Skills Challenges

Trying to make friends and meet new people can be particularly daunting if you are not naturally inclined that way or if you have disabilities. Students with social anxiety or Autism Spectrum diagnoses – as well as many others – can find the constant pressure to chat, make small talk, connect with others, and generally be sociable quite overwhelming.

Some initial top tips on taking steps towards meeting new people might include:

- Have a trusted person you can talk things through with
- Test out conversation topics with them
- Run through scenarios with them
- Get them to check in on how you're doing

Meeting people through shared interests or hobbies is always a winner, so the Welcome Week fair might feel a bit hectic. But it should give you some ideas of societies and clubs that might suit you.

Other good opportunities to meet like-minded people are through sports teams, volunteering or, of course, online – wherever you feel you can be yourself. You don't need a huge circle of friends, just a few good ones who you can rely on. Don't give up; it may take a few goes to meet them but it will be worth it.

You are *not* alone, however much you may occasionally feel it, and however "different" you may feel. There are good people out there who are keen and eager to help you. Please reach out and connect.

Remember, the uni staff are very aware of the risks of isolation, so they will be planning and arranging loads of activities for students, such as treasure hunts, pub quizzes, film nights, and so on. Some of these will not involve alcohol of course, which allows for different people to meet others with shared interests. Join any of these that might interest you, especially if they allow you to become part of a team in some way. A good example is a quiz, which is always a great way to get to know people without having to have a direct conversation.

'It's okay to not be having fun all the time, even if it looks like everyone else is. Getting involved somehow, whether that be through societies or through your course or through volunteering, is a great way to make friends and also give yourself a sense of purpose and a routine.'

Accommodation – What if You Hate it?

Where we live is absolutely crucial to our wellbeing as humans. Living in a tiny, cramped, damp space with rubbish views is soul destroying, as is being unable to sleep because of noisy neighbours or being so far from all your friends and course-mates that you can't easily join in activities. It doesn't have to be this way!

So, if you are unhappy with where you are living and it's negatively affecting your emotional wellbeing, talk to the university office or a Students' Union team that deals with these issues. If you are in private halls, speak to the inhouse manager. Make your case and see what your options are. It may not be straightforward, but there are always options, and in the first term especially there can be other students moving around or coming and going, so spaces may crop up that weren't there on arrivals day. The key here is to *talk* to someone about it in the accommodation office or private provider's office. Don't suffer in silence.

Food and Weight Issues

Arriving at uni, there is usually a choice to be made about catering options; you can usually choose catered or self-catering halls, or residences. This is clearly a personal decision, and you will need to weigh up the pros and cons of each, whether those are based on social, financial, or dietary needs.

GPs caring for thousands of students, are aware that this decision could have quite important implications for both physical and mental health. For example, if you have medical conditions requiring a special diet, such as gluten free, you will need to weigh up the cost of buying the food yourself versus asking the uni to provide it for you in a catered hall. Or, students with eating disorders might choose to live in self-catered halls, but then not actually make themselves sufficient food, leading to rapid deterioration. Neither of these scenarios are about right or wrong, they just illustrate the personal nature of this decision and the need to take time to consider your options.

It is also important not to underestimate the time it can take to cook for yourself, shop for food and so on, if you haven't done it before, as well as being able to cook a few meals, so that you can invite friends over, or just stay healthy! Resorting to takeaways and snacks can prove both expensive and unhealthy, if you realise too late that your ambition to become a world-class chef as well as study your full-time degree course may have been over-stretching your abilities a little ...

For students with eating issues, this new culinary independence can lead to challenges with staying healthy or even occasionally a deterioration in their eating. As such, if you notice this within yourself or a friend, it is important to seek advice and help without delay.

In Summary

Challenges in term one may come from accommodation issues, friendships, and academic pressures. All of these can be overcome with some help from others, including the uni's professional teams. Try to find a work-life balance and find some like-minded friends.

CHAPTER 5

TERM ONE: STAYING SAFE AND WELL

Personal Safety

Keeping yourself safe at uni is perhaps something that is lower down your list of things to think about, but it is, of course, vitally important. It can be easy to get lost in the uni "bubble" and forget that there are some dangers both inside and outside of that bubble.

Drink "spiking" – where someone else puts a substance in your drink (such as one of the "date rape" drugs or sleeping tablets) so that you become woozy, sleepy, and vulnerable to being taken advantage of or assaulted – is unfortunately a risk, and well worth being alert to.

Top Tips for Avoiding Drink Spiking

With some basic awareness and measures taken, you can protect yourself and still have a great night out:

- Never leave your drink unattended
- Never accept drinks from people unless you have watched them being poured
- Never let the drink out of your sight
- Cover your bottled drinks with your thumb or use a specially designed drink stopper that you can drink through with a straw

It is absolutely not your fault if your drink gets spiked, but it is sensible to try to reduce the risk. And if you think that you may have been at the receiving end of such a thing because you feel more drunk or woozy than you should, then tell a trusted friend or call someone you trust to take you home straightaway. Do *not* try to go home alone.

In terms of general safety when walking around or getting home at night, make sure you use reputable local transport, such as the uni buses or well-recognised cab firms (not mini cabs), and consider using one of the multiple personal safety apps that are now available. These allow your friends to see your location and track you home safely. Agree on one together, in your friendship group, and all download it so you can help each other to stay safe.

TOP TIPS

- Walk with confidence, exude an assertive manner and keep your head up, being alert to your surroundings (don't wear headphones in both ears)
- Vary your routes and avoid being predictable
- Stick to well-lit areas and try to stay with friends
- If you feel that someone is threatening you, scream 'Fire!' and attract attention if possible
- Do not walk home after a night out and make sure you have plans for safe transport home

Sexual Safety and Consent

In an ideal world, we wouldn't have to think about such things as keeping ourselves safe from sexual assault or even rape. But the world is not ideal, and without any implication of victim blaming, it is really important to do what you can to keep yourself safe from assault no matter what your gender, as it can happen to anyone.

Definition of Rape

According to the Sexual Offences Act 2003 in England and Wales, the Sexual Offences Act (Scotland) 2009 and the Sexual Offences (Northern Ireland) Order 2008*, rape is committed if:

A man (or any person of any sex, in Scotland):

- Intentionally penetrates the vagina, anus or mouth of another person (B) with their penis
- Person B does not consent to the penetration, and
- Person A does not reasonably believe that B consents.

Definition of Sexual Assault

According to the Sexual Offences Act 2003 in England and Wales, the Sexual Offences Act (Scotland) 2009 and the Sexual Offences (Northern Ireland) Order 2008*, **sexual assault** is committed if:

Person A intentionally touches another person and:

- The touching is sexual,
- Person B does not consent to the touching, and
- Person A does not reasonably believe that B consents.

*This information is up to date as of March 2019.

Huge advances have been made in recent years to raise awareness of the "consent conversation" and to bring such topics out into the open. Great resources for students are now available; they can teach you more about what consent means, and how to be a positive bystander ("bystander intervention training" teaches you how to recognise potentially harmful situations and turn them into positive outcomes by your choice of actions).

Your uni may well offer some online courses and modules in these topics and it's strongly encouraged that you take advantage of them, as well as encourage friends and flatmates to do so. The more everyone learns about it, the sooner our culture will shift to being safer for all of us.

Top Tips for Staying Sexually Safe:

- Know your sexual limits and stick to them
- Have a code word / phrase or number you can say / text to friends or family for help
- Don't be afraid to say no and hurt someone's feelings – be confident and clear or lie if necessary, to get out of the situation
- Trust your instincts and leave any situation in which you feel unsafe
- This is not your fault; don't feel pressured or allow yourself to be convinced to do anything you don't want to do
- Consent is all about communication and it can be withdrawn at any time
- Consent is a clear "yes" and *not* saying "no" does not mean you have consented to anything
- One thing does *not* have to lead to another
- Just because you have had sex with someone in the past, that does not imply consent for the next time

There is a lot more information about consent and sexual activity available on reliable websites and in the resources section of this book. But the key is to be alert to possible tricky situations. Look after yourself and your friends, and if you do need help or support after an assault then know that there are a lot of good people out there who want to help you. Help is available through your uni or local health service support teams.

Mental Health is a Thing!

It isn't uncommon for GPs to see students from all sorts of backgrounds for whom mental health had never really been recognised as the real and important issue that it is. As one student put it:

'I'm from a really conservative background and even if I knew about mental health via leaflets and websites, I don't think I would've taken it seriously because I've grown up with the idea that mental health isn't really a thing.'

This can mean that many students suffer with various symptoms – such as low or flat mood, poor sleep, anxiety, recurrent negative or difficult thoughts, self-harm, eating issues, and so on – for years without realising that they might have a mental health condition or at least an emotional difficulty that could in fact be treated or supported. They don't realise that mental health can become *ill* health in the same way that physical health can become ill health.

The Relief of Seeking and Getting Help

It can be a huge relief when students discover that what they have been feeling is a well-recognised condition with a name and treatment options, and that often the right kind of talking therapy is what is needed. Some feel enormous pressure taken off them as they try a medication they never knew existed and they "find themselves" again and a cloud of emotional negativity is lifted.

Uni may be the first time that they have spoken to someone about their symptoms. Also, as they move away from their families, and sometimes their countries or cultures, they have the opportunity to think about what is happening for them in a different light, with a different interpretation. They come to see that this is not their fault and that sometimes they have a medical condition which they cannot simply "snap out of" and can no longer ignore.

They seek advice and expert support, and new paths to recovery open up with often transformational effects.

Be open to looking for and accepting help from others, whether that's a peer or a professional. It's important to talk about mental health and make it a non-taboo subject.

Mental health *is* a thing, and is definitely worth addressing if you are suffering.

Where Can You Get Help?

The simple answer to this is to approach the university's professional student support services and ask for help, whether that is via a single point of entry "hub" or help desk, via their website, or via their counselling service.

> 'Nothing is more important than your health and wellbeing. Seeking help is the best decision and is not "weak" and you should never let academic work take priority over your wellbeing.'

You can, of course, also approach the local GP surgery or health services, and many areas have psychological services that are available for free to the general public, so search online for "free NHS local psychology services" and book yourself an assessment.

And it's free of charge! Not all students realise that uni support is free and available to all registered students.

'If you have low mood or feel suicidal, go to the doctors.'

'Use the university's mental health services, tell someone how you're feeling, don't be too hard on yourself, and give yourself a break. It's not your fault.'

'I wish I had known that mental health services were offered and were free of charge. I knew I had problems with anxiety and was receiving help before university, but I thought I would have no help at all once I started uni.'

And it's important to address this comment from a worried student:

'There *are* services available, so do not to be put off by the waiting lists. However, many, many people are still very reluctant to get help because they feel the services are so understaffed that they will have to wait ages for a session, or if they do get a session they are taking that spot away from someone else.'

There may be a wait for longer-term support, group work, or one-to-one counselling appointments, but most GP practices can see you quickly if you say it is for a mental health issue, and especially if you are feeling particularly unwell, self-harming, or suicidal.

You should never worry that other people might be more unwell than you, that you are in some way not deserving of the appointment, or that you are using up resources. That is what they are there for; they work with students because they like students and want to support them in their studies. They want to ensure that students are reaching their potential. They might well be busy, but they always want to hear from you if you are feeling unwell or suffering.

A final word from students about seeking help:

'Access everything. Try everything until you have found something that helps.'

Disabilities – Physical or Mental

In your first term, it is well worth finding out about the support available for students with disabilities and what is actually considered a disability. You may be pleasantly surprised to find that something that you have been struggling with for years, such as a mental health issue, is in fact a disability that entitles you to additional funding and help in the form of advice, mentoring, or technical support.

All universities have professionally staffed departments dedicated to supporting students with disabilities. They provide a vast array of services and advice, not just for

'I wish I had known that anxiety was actually considered to be a disability.'

learning disabilities like dyslexia, but for those with physical ill health as well as mental ill health. You may need to provide documentation from your GP or a psychologist, but once the paper work is completed the benefits can be great and really transform your experience. For example, you may be entitled to additional time for an exam, or to sit on your own to complete it.

'You should know that learning disabilities, like dyslexia, are common and any difficulties with academic skills and performance should be followed up as quickly as possible. They should be addressed with a dedicated person from the university disability team.

In Summary

Be more proactive in getting the support you need from disability and other uni services.

Term one can be a whirlwind of new experiences, so the message here is about proactive self-care. It is a crucial skill for wellbeing throughout life. Term one will throw up challenges, so take positive action and seek help from the uni's professional teams. If you are struggling, please do ask for help.

CHAPTER 6

HOLIDAYS AND SELF-CARE

Holidays

The end of the first term has arrived. You crawl, exhausted, onto the coach, train, or plane, or into the car to go home for a few weeks of well-deserved and much needed rest.

The holidays can be a wonderful opportunity to reconnect with family and friends at home, rest, eat nice food, and do a bit of revision for January exams. But they are not a haven for everyone.

For some students, going home can mean returning to a scene of conflict, to warring parents, to carer responsibilities, to controlling or abusive environments, and / or to isolation or emotional triggers. Not all homes are warm, welcoming, and supportive.

Students have told GPs about their medication being thrown away by upset parents who have discovered their mental health pills. They've told of refusals to acknowledge their psychological condition as a "real thing". Students may come from a culture where their lifestyle or personal choices are frowned upon or where they feel unable to be themselves with regards to gender or sexuality issues.

Conflicting Emotions

Returning home can bring up all sorts of conflicting emotions, from the very significant to the more mundane, for example wanting to be treated as an adult but having your parents treat you as the child you were when you left home.

In the latter situation, it can help to bring this up in a non-confrontational way with specific examples, such as the time you might like to come home after a night out (if that has caused discussion) while offering to do things to help around the house such as food shopping, laundry, and so on. This way you're not treating the family home like the hall of residence or a hotel.

Being thoughtful about how you fit back into the home when your family may only just have adjusted to your absence can help, along with spending time with other relatives, checking how your family are feeling, and asking how life is for them. Things may have changed or been difficult since you left, but they may have avoided sharing this with you so as not to distract you from your studies.

The key to a successful holiday period – if there are not significant issues such as those relating to severe disagreement over gender, sexuality, or personal issues – is to spend time together *and* apart, to give everyone space to adjust while having time to catch up and allow the family dynamics to equilibrate. Be thoughtful, help out, and be sensitive to other people's feelings.

Assuming that is all going well, the holidays can be a time to recover from the extremes of diet (and alcohol), sleep disturbance, and the general assault on the human body that is student life, with a bit of self-care.

It's time to get back in shape, eat fresh food, exercise, and get fit for the term ahead!

What if You Don't or Can't "Go Home" for the Holidays?

There can be various reasons why students don't leave uni at holiday times. They may not have a home to return to; perhaps they've been in care or are homeless. They could be international students for whom it is too expensive or challenging to travel. Maybe they'd rather avoid a conflict or difficult scenario, or perhaps their room at home is now in use by someone else, leaving them without a place to stay.

The university will likely be able to help support all these students in different ways, *if they are made aware of the situation*. They can often arrange homestays with local families, accommodation in residences, trips to enjoy local activities such as Christmas markets, day-to-day support from uni welfare or chaplaincy staff, and social media groups for all the students to link up if they wish to connect with others in the same circumstances.

The key here is that if you would like to connect with others, over the holidays, and keep busy or try something new, then talk to the university support services *in advance* and allow them to help you achieve that.

Self-Care

> 'Schedule a few hours in, spread over each week, where you do something active or self-care-ish that isn't remotely related to your course.'

Great advice, for both term time and holidays, of course, so ...

Let's Play Self-Care Bingo!

For this activity you need to draw a 5 x 5 (3 x 3 is fine too!) square card like this:

Then think of things that make you feel happy, warm, contented, energised, relaxed, and so on. Write them in the squares. For example, "Listen to a podcast or [name of song]", "Bake fairy cakes", "Watch box set / Netflix", "Do a home manicure", "Work out with a punchbag" or "Go outside".

I'm sure you can think of lots more that are personal to you and will lift your spirits. They might involve other people too, so you might include "Call a friend", or "Go for a walk with [friend's name]". Petting your dog or hamster counts too!

Once you have created your bingo card you can put it somewhere ready for days back at uni too, when you might need a little more support or feel a bit down or alone. You can play by choosing which activities you feel like doing that day. If you have a good friend, they can play too, with the aim of focusing on having a day that lifts the spirits and feels good.

In Summary

Looking after yourself is important, and there are lots of practical ways that you can do this. It's important to remember that uni life is not just about term time either, and that the holidays can bring their own challenges. They are not necessarily full of fun family or travel experiences and they're not always easy to fill with internships and great CV-related opportunities. Sometimes getting through the holidays is a job in itself, and preparing for that possibility may help you to manage that task a little more easily.

CHAPTER 7

TERM TWO

Term two at uni can be a roller coaster of activities.

Exams, deadlines, assignments, new activities, thinking about housing for next year – all of these pressures and more can suddenly pile up if you're not ready, looking after yourself and firing on all cylinders.

The key to success here is pacing yourself, preparation, and sleep!

Sleep

'Make sure you have a balance of time with others and time by yourself, and get enough sleep.'

We all underestimate the importance of sleep.

'A good night's shut-eye can make us cleverer, more attractive, slimmer, happier, healthier and ward off cancer.'
Mark O'Connell (Guardian)

Missing out on sleep can have a "catastrophic effect" on your health and wellbeing. And GPs often tell students that rather than resort to study drugs as many do (to stay awake and work longer), they would be better off getting a good night's sleep and then having a cup of coffee in the morning.

So How Do You Get a Good Night's Sleep?

Well first of all, before we get into the "sleep rules", it's important to understand that sleep is a habit. And so, if it has been "broken" and you are not sleeping well, or you have been sleeping in the day and up all night, then it will take time to reset your "biological clock" and get into a good habit. About six weeks of following the sleep rules should do it, but if you're still struggling after that, talk to a doctor or therapist about it. Don't suffer in silence.

Insomnia and disrupted sleep patterns can be absolute torture, as junior doctors and others who go for days without sleep and work nights will tell you. You are strongly urged not to ignore this essential bodily function!

TOP TIPS

The Rules

- Try to go to bed and get up at the same time every day, Monday to Sunday. If necessary, use your alarm to set the routine!
- Try to be asleep when it's dark and awake when it's light, although within reason, for example between 11.00pm and 8.00am, but not sleeping in the daytime or staying up all night to work. You need about nine hours sleep on average as a young adult.
- If you have to nap in the day, then do it before 3.00pm.
- Stop all work and turn off all screens one hour before bedtime.
- Spend that hour winding down, chatting with a friend, listening to quiet music, having a hot bath, reading quietly, or watching TV (nothing too scary or exciting!).
- Exercise in the daytime before about 6.00pm, and don't have caffeine or alcohol late in the evening nor eat any heavy meals. Light snacks are okay.

- Create a gadget-free zone – lights that might blink at night, notifications lighting up the room, and clocks that you can stare at are all no-nos.
- Don't lie in bed awake for hours. If you can't get off to sleep, get up and do a relaxing activity for a while. When you feel sleepier, try again to sleep.
  (medlineplus.gov, 2012)

Stick to these rules for about 4–6 weeks, and if that isn't working check out CBT-I (Cognitive Behavioural Therapy for Insomnia). It is evidence-based and designed to improve sleep. Also make time to talk to a professional about how you are doing. There may be other things you can try that can help to improve your sleep and mood.

Exercise

Look, it's not exactly news that exercise is good for us, or that we should try to stay active on a regular basis. Life is too short to repeat the obvious and tell you what you already know. But in terms of uni life and being a student, even the most dedicated school athletes can find it hard to stay fit once they hit the campus!

Universities provide a huge range of opportunities for exercise, sport, and activity, ranging from top-level teams to beginners. Many are showcased at Welcome Week fair of course, but you can check them out all year round. Residences and the Students' Union will host groups and classes, whether you're into Zumba or historical walking tours. The choices are endless, and hopefully there is something for everyone (including women-only classes if that is a priority for you), but if you are not naturally inclined to breaking into a sweat or moving at faster than a gentle stroll, at least make it easy for yourself:

TOP TIPS

- Take the stairs rather than the lifts
- Walk or cycle instead of taking the bus or driving
- If you have to sit at a desk all day or be in lectures for long hours, then make sure you take breaks to get outside and walk around the block at the very least

Screen Time

We all spend a lot of time on our phones, and many of us likely have a love–hate relationship with the technology that surrounds us daily.

No one is suggesting that you stop using your phone, iPad, or laptop, but it may be worth taking a moment to reflect on *how much* you use it, what your attention span is like, and what you could be doing instead of being on your screen, with the aim of perhaps studying better and achieving more with your time.

Studies have shown that 17-year-olds spend around six hours a day of their leisure time (not studying) on their screens (Monitoring the Future, 2013–2015), and that their attention span is about 19 seconds on average before they switch tasks on their laptops (Yeykelis, Cummings and Reeves, 2014).

Take a moment to reflect on those facts and compare your own screen time. You may want to consider spending some of that texting / surfing / video chatting time on activities with other humans, reading, or doing something active that will make you feel better emotionally. You might also like to try using tech to control your tech use, such as apps to reduce or manage your screen time if necessary.

The Effects of More Screen Time on Our Lives

Sadly, research is finding that *the more time we spend on our screens, the less happy we are*. More screen time causes more anxiety, depression, loneliness and less emotional connection (Tromholt, 2016 and Sherman, Michikyan and Greenfield, 2013). It also makes us more likely to be overweight.

On the other hand, spending time with other humans face-to-face makes us feel better, happier, and healthier.

It is important of course to acknowledge the significant support many people also draw on via online groups, social media, and networks, to keep themselves from being isolated or to meet those with shared interests. Screen time is absolutely *not all bad*, but as with most things in life, a little bit of balance goes a long way.

So every now and then give yourself a break, get out and see actual people, connect with the outside world. Take time to read books (to improve your attention span), and exercise, which will in turn help you to study more effectively for your degree.

Smoking

GPs often find that trying to get students to give up smoking when they have often only just started is *really* hard!

Students definitely smoke in fewer numbers these days, which is great because it really is bad for your health in so many ways (it damages your lungs, heart, kidneys, eyes, brain ... the list goes on) but some students obviously do still smoke and often it is used as a stress relief mechanism. So if you are a smoker, then maybe it is worth having a think about *why* you smoke, and whether there might be a healthier alternative.

You could also think about the money you would save, and put it towards something specific, so that it really does feel like a positive achievement when you quit and have some cash (or a treat) to show for it!

Help to give up smoking is available through your doctor's surgery, so ask at reception or look for your local Stop Smoking Service for free on the NHS website.

You are more likely to be successful at giving up smoking with support or professional help, so take the time to look after yourself and book yourself an appointment at a time when you don't feel too stressed and are ready to make the change (i.e., not right before exams!).

Drugs

Students use drugs for many different reasons – to party, sure, but also to self-medicate (to help with their own distress, anxiety, depression, and so on), to cope with exam stress specifically, to study (see below re study drugs) and to manage social anxiety, to name but a few.

The offer of drugs may come at any time of course, although I have put it into the Term Two chapter because this may be when it actually becomes a problem, rather than just fun. When the work is piling up, the exams become real, the deadlines loom, past drug use can seem like a mistake you wish you'd never made, and future drug use may seem like an option to help you cope. However, if you are struggling with your wellbeing or you are under pressure with work, then, as one of my students said very clearly, 'Don't drink. Don't go anywhere near drugs.'

So, if this is the situation for you and you are stressed, try to avoid using any drugs and talk to someone about getting help. Get into a healthy daily sleep and exercise routine. Eat some fresh food daily, and make a study timetable you can follow, maybe with a friend, to keep you on track and feeling like *you can do this*.

If you are using drugs and are finding it hard to stop but you would like to, you are not alone. It's hard to get a real sense of how common drug use is among UK university students, with two studies in 2018 giving differing results. The NUS report *Taking the Hit* showed that 56 per cent of 3,000 respondents had ever used drugs, but the Higher Education

Policy Institute (HEPI) report of 1,000 students showed only 39% had. More interesting perhaps were the differing attitudes of the students in the two surveys about whether or not drug use is harmful to mental health. Despite a mountain of scientific evidence to the contrary (drugabuse.gov), two-thirds of NUS respondents who thought that drug use had affected their health said it had done so in a positive way, improving their mental health.

The fact is that drugs are not good for you, and if you are using them to cope with stress or anxiety then please talk to a professional healthcare worker. They are there to help you with whatever underlying issues are causing your worries. They want to help you to deal with them in a healthier and more effective way.

Mid-Term Blues

Whether they happen in term one or two, the mid-term blues are all too real for some students. You hit the ground running as term starts, full of energy, drive, enthusiasm, and ideas, then as the weeks progress you slump, overcome with exhaustion, burning the candle at both ends, and too tired to do anything properly. It can be a bit of a shock, but it's common and nothing to panic about.

This is a good moment to review that self-care bingo we talked about, and designed, before. Plan a few early nights to get your sleep pattern back on track, or book a day out of your diary to just do things that you enjoy and don't involve any work.

Take a Day Off!

Taking a break from work can be essential to allow your brain to recover from all the revision, exams, and essays, to think in new ways about work or projects, and approach your next assignment feeling refreshed.

If you think you might need help to plan your workload or manage all the competing demands, then ask your personal tutor or someone in your academic department for help. Check out what study skills workshops and learning events are being held.

If the uni only has "one job" then this is it. They are there to help get your degree, so take advantage of all their resources and get the support you need!

In Summary

Term two can be more of a bumpy ride than you might have expected, so it's really important to keep to a good sleep routine, exercise when you can, and if you have been coping with the stress or "self-medicating" by gaming online, smoking, or taking drugs of any sort, then please take some time to sort yourself out and look after yourself.

If you're feeling the pressure and it's starting to affect you and your work, then help is out there – including from the uni support services, your academic tutors and department staff, and your family and friends, as well as online and in books. You are not alone, so please do reach out.

CHAPTER 8

TERM THREE

When you think about the summer term, exams are probably the main thing on your mind, but perhaps you also start to think about holidays, jobs, next year's potential flatmate issues, graduation, study years abroad, and so on. All of these things can bring both a sense of achievement and a sense of adventure ... or possibly anxiety.

You've made it this far. The end of the academic year is in sight and a new chapter is about to begin. But for some it can feel a bit overwhelming; the fear of failing the exams is high and the worry about change (nobody likes change!) is real and can make you nervous.

Flatmate Issues

On the subject of next year's housing, it can be worth taking a moment to consider the issues that can arise with housemates. Uni is a unique opportunity to meet people from all over the world, from multiple cultural and societal backgrounds, and it can be a fantastic way to make new friends.

When you move in together, it can test those friendships in a way that hanging out in the bar or living in halls never did. Suddenly you have bills to pay together, cleaning to do, maintenance to be aware of, and responsibilities – and not everyone shares the same attitudes and values towards these important (if dull!) tasks. Despite the plethora of amusing blogs about clichéd flatmate stereotypes, it can sometimes cause a serious degree of stress, not least if a friend has a mental health issue which can then impact on other housemates.

Flatmates with Mental Health Issues

If this is a scenario you are concerned about, talk to someone about it (preferably a member of the university mental health teams) and get advice. You are not the person's carer or next of kin, and other people need to help you to support them. As a friend you don't have a confidentiality boundary, nor should you feel pressured to keep things secret. Please talk to the professionals if you need help.

If the flatmate issues are more related to differing approaches to rent / bills / care of the property / partying habits and so on, then think carefully about how to approach the tricky housemate and use your best "conflict resolution" skills to have a difficult conversation.

Top Tips on Addressing Conflict

- Find a calm time and place to talk
- Use active listening (really hear what they are saying and try not to judge them)
- Be fair
- Solve the problem and don't attack each other
- Accept responsibility
- Be direct
- Find common ground
- Try to find a shared future aim or solution (where do you both want to be?)
- Agree your mutual shared benefit (negotiate / compromise)
- If you can't compromise, maybe agree to differ and move on

- If the conversation gets too heated, take time out and come back to it

Using this approach might avoid the breakdown of a good friendship and pre-empt a difficult situation.

Pre-Exam Panic

Remember! The third term can be a stressful time and you are not alone. Pre-exam season can be a particularly fraught time for students, so make use of any revision classes, extra seminars or lectures, groups for study skills, or de-stressing sessions involving sport or even puppies! They are all there to help you succeed and stay well.

Even if you think you have left it too late to get help and that no one can help you now, it is genuinely never too late.

Universities have systems in place to aid and assist students whatever the situation, and even if you might need to take time out and re-sit a year, you would be one of many, *many* students who do this each year. Similarly, if you are ill on the day of an exam or during your exam, as long as you let people know and engage with the processes, there are plenty of options to solve the problem.

Study Drugs

It's at this point that you may, if you haven't already, consider trying study drugs or "smart" drugs.

Revision feels like a mountain to climb, there aren't enough hours in the day, exams are looming, and deadlines feel far too real. The idea of using something to "boost" your performance would hardly be new, and it's believed that James Bond, JFK, and Hitler were all fans of using prescription medications in non-prescription ways to increase their alertness or effectiveness.

However, taking prescription medications when they have not been prescribed for you, or for a purpose other than which they were designed for, brings significant risks. For example, students sometimes take medication designed to treat those with diagnosed Attention Deficit Disorder in the mistaken belief that it will allow them to improve the quality of their work, study more effectively, write a better essay, and so on. The evidence to date shows that in healthy individuals functioning at optimum level, these (and other "smart" medications) will make *no improvement* to cognitive functioning and may in fact impair performance (BMA.org. uk, 2015).

Students also commonly take a medication usually used for narcolepsy (when you fall asleep spontaneously at inappropriate times) to keep them awake for excessive periods of time, to allow them to work for longer. They will definitely keep you awake for a long time, but as we have mentioned before, sleep deprivation is bad for your health and can even lead to hallucinations, among other side effects. Sleep is also crucial for your memory to function.

Needless to say, these medications have significant side effects and possibly long-term complications in those for whom they have not been prescribed. It is these unpleasant side effects that usually bring students to GPs' consulting rooms: palpitations, diarrhoea, headaches, and an inability to sleep at all.

So when someone offers you a "quick fix" to "boost" your study, bear this in mind: it is risky, potentially dangerous, and – most ironic of all – "smart" drugs don't make you smarter!

Another quick word about alcohol – it is really normal for humans to find ways to cope when things are difficult, and we all use a variety of "substances" with which to "self-medicate." Food, cigarettes, drugs and alcohol are all common sources of distraction for us when we are stressed. If you notice that you are starting to "use" any of these more or relying on them to get you through challenging times, try to stop and ask yourself *why* you are needing them. There will be other things you can do instead that might be better, such as exercise, talking to friends and family about your stress, or relaxation techniques.

Exams, Assignments, and Academic Pressure

Clearly academic pressure will have been something to think about before the summer term, but it's covered here because this is when GPs see the most students about work-related worries and stress.

When Does Academic Stress Warrant Intervention?

First of all, it is important to say that it is entirely normal to feel anxious and worried about exams. Our bodies are designed to give us a rush of adrenaline when we are stressed, to help focus the mind and be on our toes. So there is no need to worry about worrying!

If, however, you feel more than manageably anxious (for example, if you haven't slept for days, you have stopped eating, you are losing weight, you cry all the time, you no longer enjoy the activities you did before, and so on) then please do talk with a professional about how you are feeling. This will give you a sense of whether you have moved beyond normal anxiety about work to being unwell and requiring help.

You don't need to see a GP or counsellor if you can't sleep the night before a specific exam, if you feel sick just before it, or if you feel on edge about it. This is all very normal and there's nothing we can do. But if you are shaking and sweating and having palpitations and are physically a bit overwhelmed by your "fight or flight" reaction, it may be worth discussing this "performance related anxiety". You could consider learning relaxation techniques or even taking beta blockers (which don't cloud the mind, but block the adrenaline that is rushing to your sweat glands, and so on).

And Most Serious of All ... Suicide Risk

There is no doubt that students worry about money, making friends, and eating healthily among other things, but academic stress looms very large for many and can sadly even be a factor in student suicide, with rates of suicide peaking in exam months such as April and May (NCISH, 2018).

This underlines how important it is not to ignore your distress if you are finding work or life overwhelming, worried about letting people down, or frightened of "failure".

There is *always* something that the uni support services, health teams, and counsellors can do to help, so even if *you* have never considered what all the options are, it is likely that they will have come across a similar situation before and will be able to offer hope and a practical plan.

I need help NOW!

Immediate help is always available if you feel like this. Dial the emergency phone number 999, speak to your doctor, or go to the local hospital emergency department. Organisations like Samaritans are also available 24 / 7, by phone or text. (Tel 116 123 free call.)

Top Tips for Exam Preparation

- Don't leave it all till the last minute – plan your revision and stick to the plan.
- Use flow charts, diagrams, and visual aids – people learn brilliantly with images to help them.
- Practise old exam papers and questions.
- Explain topics to people who don't study them with you; having to explain something helps you to understand it better.

- Take breaks for 10 minutes at least. Stretch, walk, get outside, and get some vitamin D every 60–90 minutes.
- Eat sensible healthy food and stay hydrated. And don't skip breakfast on the day of the exam!
- Plan for the day of the exam. Where and when is it happening? (Yes, GPs have been asked for a note by someone who missed their exam because they "got lost on the way". But no, they didn't write one!)
- Get lots of sleep the night before.
- Vary the location of your revision for most effective learning (Carey, 2015) and reduced anxiety sitting the exam in an unfamiliar location.
- Don't just copy out lecture notes – read them, then write down what you remember for better long-term recall.
- Work in a group and explain things to each other, if you like studying with others.

Summer Holidays

You've made it!

You've survived the year, the exams and the emotional roller coaster that university can be.

And here you are, ready for the holidays.

As we said in the chapter about holidays in general, many students may look upon the summer with apprehension rather than anticipation, but for everyone it will likely bring a change of routine, a change of scene perhaps, and opportunity to earn money, travel, see old friends, and catch up with family. But it may also bring a feeling of unease or worry.

Students who have happily discovered their identity at uni and been accepted as themselves may not be the person their family remembers, and there may be resulting conflict or some adaptation required on both sides.

It may be difficult to take a new romantic partner home with you or to explain your sexuality to those who have known you since childhood.

Whatever the scenario, it is important to think ahead as term progresses, as the summer term is notoriously short, and the holidays will arrive before you think it possible.

TOP TIPS

Preparing for the Summer Break

- Apply for internships and jobs well in advance
- Drop hints about any changes in you or your lifestyle to those back home
- Make travel plans
- Think ahead to the next academic year, even if the basics, like accommodation and course modules, are in place
- It may be worth speaking to those in the year above you and asking for any top tips and what they wish they had known in advance

There are many things you can do if you feel like the holidays are stretching ahead and you're not too sure what to do. It doesn't have to be ice cream and Netflix all the way, though that is obviously fine for your days off!

Other Summer Activities

Think about volunteering at a local charity. It will be great experience, help you meet people, and give you something to put on that all-important CV.

If you can, learn to drive and get independent. It's a life skill and is particularly useful for some careers too.

Apply to get work experience somewhere that interests you, especially if you're not too sure what you want to do with your life. For example, do you wonder what it would be like to be a music therapist or a veterinary nurse? Then contact local people who do these roles and ask if you can shadow them or even just have a chat if it's too complicated to go into their workplace.

You can always make a start on any course reading lists for next year and plan a couple of festival visits (not necessarily the big expensive ones) with friends while you decide what to do with the rest of your break.

The summer holidays are a great opportunity to take a break, recover from uni life, get your health back, travel long distances to see the world, or earn a decent bit of cash for the year ahead. But most of all, you've earned them!

In Summary

Term three can be short, but nevertheless it can bring its own difficulties. Exams are the main stress for most students, though flatmates and holiday or graduation plans can run a close second. It is really important not to underestimate how much pressure students can feel at exam time and it can have a particularly significant effect on mental health. So, if you are struggling, you are most definitely not alone and it is *never* too late to seek support and advice.

Don't ignore the stress or believe that no one can help you now. And if you are feeling desperate or you're even thinking about suicide, then the support teams and healthcare professionals particularly want to reach out to you and tell you that there is *always* hope, that the university *can* help you, and that compassionate (uni or health service) professionals are always available if you ask for help.

CHAPTER 9

IN SUMMARY

In summary, you're at uni to get a degree and have a good time doing it, while hopefully making some new friends and learning some new skills. Universities are there to make sure that you achieve these things to the best of your ability, to help you fulfil your potential, and move on in the world having had a positive experience.

This book is to support you in achieving these things while staying healthy and knowing a little bit more about how to stay well (and safe) at uni.

A little preparation before arrival, knowing more what to expect of each term, and understanding that sometimes things don't always play out quite as you'd expect (for example, the holidays) will mean that you can navigate your first year at uni ready to study effectively, connect with other people, care for yourself and, importantly, have some fun!

Uni life may not be the "best days of your life" but it is a real opportunity to try new things, find your "tribe", stretch yourself, perhaps discover a secret talent and get a degree before you embark on your next adventure.

Five Ways to Wellbeing / Staying Well

This is another great way to think about how to look after yourself all year round, but it's great to start practising in the holidays when you have the brain space to think about it.

The Five Ways to Wellbeing were suggested a few years ago by the New Economics Foundation (Gov.uk, 2008), and set out the five things we can all do to stay well:

1. **Connect** – this relates to connecting with other people. We are social creatures, and as humans we do best when connected to others in positive ways.

2. **Be active** – staying active and exercising – even if it's just walking or strolling – is highly recommended for a healthy life.

3. **Take notice** – this refers to being aware of the world around you, of nature, of the activities you do, of your breathing, of what you eat. It is often associated with the practice of mindfulness (taking time to focus on the present moment and appreciate the sensations associated with it).

4. **Keep learning** – a good one for uni students, this is about keeping your brain active and healthy by always being curious and learning new things.

5. **Give** – this relates to the fact that helping others makes you feel better and happier too. So take the time to volunteer, help a friend, share, and so on.

In reality, this way of approaching self-care and wellbeing means looking for ways to spend time with other people and finding activities that you enjoy. It doesn't mean making yourself train for marathons if you hate running, but it can mean going for a lovely walk outside, somewhere you enjoy. That might be a park, the woods, the beach, a market, or any big open space where you can see the sky. It is also about being aware of the world around you as you wander – the smells, the sounds, the colours, the feel of the ground under your feet, the touch of leaves on trees, or clothes on stalls. It's about taking time to appreciate the world around you, reconnecting with it, and being in that moment.

You could also look for ways to help and support others. That might be by giving your time or sharing your energy or abilities by volunteering locally. Hopefully, as a student, the aim to "keep learning" will be a given, but you might want to add something else into the mix. You could learn a new language, instrument, activity, or skill. It's up to you, but all of these ways to stay well should lift your spirits and keep you feeling enthusiastic and on track for the new term.

Getting Help and Resources

DAY-TO-DAY TOP TIPS

- Talk to family or friends for support.
- There are lots of self-help options available: exercise, being around nature, nurturing a pet or plant, connecting with others and helping them too, as well as mindfulness techniques if you need a bit of "me time". You'll feel good for trying and there's always more help if you are struggling.
- Your uni will provide loads of free help, for example via the counselling, chaplaincy or wellbeing services.
- Check in with the Disability team to see if you are entitled to support.
- Use the free student counselling service at your uni – every UK university has one.
- Look at your uni doctor's practice (GP Surgery) or your university's Student Support services website as a first step to see what they can offer.
- If you are an international student, look out for the International Student Office.
- Uni residences and halls will usually have staff and peer support teams focused on your wellbeing.
- Peer mentors are hard at work in most universities, students supporting other students.

- Many universities offer free online support too, so that's another option to consider if you aren't keen to talk face-to-face.
- The Students' Union is a great place to look for groups, clubs, societies, and wellbeing advice and help.
- Don't forget that the security teams are available and often trained in mental health support. They are there to protect you and advise on personal safety. Some universities have their very own police officer!
- The sports, exercise and health teams in most universities are really active and keen to get students involved, whether for specific teams, individual sports, or general activities to stay healthy.
- On the academic side, your personal tutor should be the first port of call, the person to talk to if your work is worrying you or if there is anything you want to discuss. If they can't help you directly then they can signpost you to the right person, give advice, and listen and be proactive.
- Your academic department will also be home to lots of lovely administrative staff who spend a lot of their time helping students. They will be a source of a huge variety of useful knowledge, so make sure you meet them early on and chat with them when you can – if they are not too busy at that moment.
- The careers team can help with student jobs and holiday work as well as long-term career planning.

10 TOP TRANSITION AND WELLBEING TIPS FOR NEW STUDENTS STARTING UNI

1. **Prepare:** Sit down with someone you trust and write a list of all your worries and concerns, so that you can start to address them together.

2. **Create an action plan:** Put all your worries or concerns into different categories, such as making friends, your studies, budgeting, living away from home and make an action plan for each one, containing solutions for each worry.

3. **Organise your medical care:** If you need support for any health condition or disability, plan how you can get the care and support you need. A good starting point is to search your university's website for 'student support' to look for information about available services.

4. **Register with a new GP:** Check out your university's website to see if they have a surgery on campus or whether they recommend a particular GP practice. Phone the new GP practice and see if they have anyone who specialises in student health. If you have mental or physical health issues, make the call yourself if you can. If you find it hard, ask your next of kin to call and sit next to them so you can listen and join in if needed.

5. **Medication:** If you take regular medicines or need medical devices or equipment, plan what you need and get an appropriate supply of prescriptions in advance (to be agreed with your GP) so you don't run out!

6. **Contact Student Support:** If you have ongoing mental health issues, get in touch with Student Support before you go to Uni. They're there to support you and will do what they can to help. Phone or email them for advice and don't be shy in asking for help if you need it.

7. **Sort out ongoing care:** If you're under specialist care for conditions like asthma, diabetes or a mental health problem, register with a new GP as soon as possible so that you can discuss ongoing care and possible referral to local services.

8. **Get comfortable:** Take a few things with you that remind you of home, like a dressing gown or your usual duvet and bedsheets instead of buying new ones. You could

also make a playlist of your favourite songs and photos of family and friends for times when you need a boost.

9. **Look after your wellbeing:** Make a Personal Wellbeing Plan of five things you can do every day and to help build your wellbeing. Include things in your plan like sleep, exercise, activities that you enjoy, something relaxing, socialising with friends, small treats, Uniclubs, support from home, and so on.

10. **Make a Safety Plan:** Sit down with someone you trust and make a plan of things you can do for yourself. Write down how you can get in touch with people you can ask for support if you ever feel low, get stressed or are struggling.

If you're worried or stressed after reading our tips please talk to someone about how you are feeling as you may need extra support.

Tips provided by **Dr Alys Cole-King** (@AlysColeKing) with input from **Dr Dom Thompson**, Student Health Expert (@DrDomThompson | buzzconsulting.co.uk) and **Dr Knut Schroeder** (@DrKnutand @expertselfcare)

10 TOP TIPS FOR PARENTS SENDING THEIR CHILD OFF TO UNIVERSITY

1. **Cooking:** Teach them how to cook. Start with two or three simple recipes they can cook for themselves and others, which can help them make new friends.

2. **Laundry:** Teach them how to do their laundry. It's a simple and essential life-skill – and it saves your own time!

3. **Healthcare:** Teach them where to get over-the-counter medicines and prescriptions, how to register and book a GP appointment and how to navigate NHS if they're unwell.

4. **Budget:** Plan a budget for food shopping and other essentials. Instead of organising food delivery, let them learn for themselves how to shop sensibly. Useful financial tips for students are available at www.blackbullion.com.

5. **First aid:** Teach them basic first aid and provide them with a small kit containing essentials like plasters, bandages, dressings, paper stitches and painkillers.

6. **Security:** Explain basic security measures, such as avoiding using cashpoints at night, protecting drinks so they don't get spiked and keeping belongings safe. Ask them to download a mobile security app such as Companion.

7. **Parental contacts:** Agree and plan in advance how often you'll contact each other and which medium you'll use, such as weekly phone calls or WhatsApp messages every other day. Allow some flexibility and don't expect daily contacts, so you won't get stressed if they oversleep and didn't check in.

8. **Drop-off:** Don't hang around too long when dropping them off. They need to get on and meet people and start blending in, not be worrying about you.

9. **Biscuits:** Take biscuits or cake (ideally low-sugar and low-fat –with gluten and nut free options) when dropping them off to create an instant talking point with other new students and their parents.

10. **Coming home:** Allow at least four weeks before they come home, so they can meet people and don't miss out on early events that help them build connections that are key to feeling settled and part of the wider university community.

Tips provided by **Dr Dom Thompson**, Student Health Expert (@DrDomThompson | buzzconsulting.co.uk) with input from **Dr Alys Cole-King** (@AlysColeKing) and **Dr Knut Schroeder** (@ DrKnutand @expertselfcare)

CHAPTER 10

WHERE CAN I FIND OUT MORE?

If you need other sorts of resources, online or books then here is a list to get you started, as there is a massive amount of info for students out there.

Apps

- *Student Health App* – for all health matters
- Personal safety apps
- CBT-I apps – for insomnia
- *distrACT* – for self-harm
- *Headspace* – for mindfulness
- *SAM app* – for anxiety

Websites

- *Know Before You Go*
  www.studentminds.org.uk / knowbeforeyougo.html
- NHS support **www.nhs.uk**
- Financial advice **Blackbullion.com**
- Financial advice **MoneySavingExpert.com**
- Financial advice **Savethestudent.org**
- The Mix **www.themix.org.uk**
- Mind **www.mind.org.uk** or call **0300 123 3393**
- Moodgym (for CBT skills) **www.moodgym.com.au**
- Student Minds (the UK national student mental health charity) **www.studentminds.org.uk**

- Drug info **www.talktofrank.com**
- Alcohol info **www.drinkaware.co.uk**
- Addiction **www.addaction.org.uk**
- Gambling and gaming **www.gamequitters.com** and **www.gamanon.org.uk**
- Eating issues **www.network-ed.org.uk**
- ADHD **www.adhdfoundation.org.uk**
- Asperger's **www.autism.org.uk**
- Gender issues **www.mermaidsuk.org.uk**
- LGBT+ **www.stonewall.org.uk**

Books

- *How We Learn* by Benedict Carey
- *Study Skills Handbook* by Stella Cottrell
- *Why We Sleep* by Matthew Walker
- *Social Media and Mental Health: Handbook for Teens* by Dr Claire Edwards
- *Social Media and Mental Health: Handbook for Parents and Guardians* by Dr Claire Edwards

YouTube

- Pooky Knightsmith on Mental Health videos

REFERENCES

Assets.publishing.service.gov.uk. (2018). *STIs and screening for chlamydia in England 2017*. [online] Available at: https://assets.publishing.service.gov.uk/government/uploads/system/uploads/attachment_data/file/713944/hpr2018_AA-STIs_v5.pdf [Accessed 16 Nov. 2018].

Bma.org.uk. (2015). *BMA - Cognitive enhancing drugs and the workplace*. [online] Available at: https://www.bma.org.uk/advice/employment/occupational-health/cognitive-enhancing-drugs [Accessed 12 Dec. 2018].

Drugabuse.gov. (2017). *Mental Health Effects*. [online] Available at: https://www.drugabuse.gov/publications/health-consequences-drug-misuse/mental-health-effects [Accessed 12 Dec. 2018].

GOV.UK. (2008). *Five ways to mental wellbeing*. [online] Available at: https://www.gov.uk/government/publications/five-ways-to-mental-wellbeing [Accessed 10 Dec. 2018].

HEPI. (2018). *Most students think taking illegal drugs causes problems for users as well as society and want their universities to take a tougher stance - HEPI*. [online] Available at: https://www.hepi.ac.uk/2018/06/12/students-think-taking-illegal-drugs-causes-problems-users-well-society-want-universities-take-tougher-stance/ [Accessed 12 Dec. 2018].

Holloway, K. and Bennett, T. (2017). Characteristics and correlates of drug use and misuse among university students in Wales: a survey of seven universities. *Addiction Research & Theory*, 26(1), pp.11-19.

Hughes, G., Massey, F. and Williams, S. (2017). *An investigation of the views, understanding, knowledge, experience and attitudes of sixth form teachers in regard to the preparedness of their students for the transition to university.* [online] Derby.openrepository.com. Available at: http://derby.openrepository.com/derby/handle/10545/621721 [Accessed 13 Nov. 2018].

John, E. (2017). *Adult drinking habits in Great Britain - Office for National Statistics.* [online] Ons.gov.uk. Available at: https://www.ons.gov.uk/peoplepopulationandcommunity/healthandsocialcare/drugusealcoholandsmoking/bulletins/opinionsandlifestylesurveyadultdrinkinghabits ingreatbritain/2017 [Accessed 16 Nov. 2018].

Medlineplus.gov. (2012). **Tips for Getting A Good Night's Sleep | NIH MedlinePlus the Magazine**. [online] Available at: https://medlineplus.gov/magazine/issues/summer15/articles/summer15pg22.html [Accessed 12 Dec. 2018].

NCISH. (2018). *Annual report 2018: England, Northern Ireland, Scotland and Wales - NCISH.* [online] Available at: https://sites.manchester.ac.uk/ncish/reports/annual-report-2018-england-northern-ireland-scotland-and-wales/ [Accessed 12 Dec. 2018].

Nus.org.uk. (2018). *New survey shows trends in student drinking.* [online] Available at: https://www.nus.org.uk/en/news/press-releases/new-survey-shows-trends-in-student-drinking/ [Accessed 16 Nov. 2018].

Nusdigital.s3-eu-west-1.amazonaws.com. (2018). *Taking the Hit: student drug use and how institutions respond.* [online] Available at: https://www.nusconnect.org.uk/resources/taking-the-hit-student-drug-use-and-how-institutions-respond [Accessed 12 Dec. 2018].

Sherman, L., Michikyan, M. and Greenfield, P. (2013). *The effects of text, audio, video, and in-person communication* on bonding between friends. [online] Available at: https://cyberpsychology.eu/article/view/4285 [Accessed 12 Dec. 2018].

Studentminds.org.uk. (2018). *Know before you go*. [online] Available at: https://www.studentminds.org.uk/uploads/3/7/8/4/3784584/180813_kbyg_interactive.pdf [Accessed 13 Nov. 2018].

Thompson, D. and Cole-King, A. (2018). *10 top transition and wellbeing tips for new students starting uni*. [online] Connectingwithpeople.org. Available at: http://connectingwithpeople.org/blogroll [Accessed 13 Nov. 2018].

Tromholt, M. (2016). *The Facebook Experiment: Quitting Facebook Leads to Higher Levels of Well-Being*. – PubMed - NCBI. [online] Ncbi.nlm.nih.gov. Available at: https://www.ncbi.nlm.nih.gov/pubmed/27831756 [Accessed 12 Dec. 2018].

Waters, L. (2018). **Putting the rise of STIs in England into context**. [online] Pharmaceutical Journal. Available at: https://www.pharmaceutical-journal.com/opinion/insight/putting-the-rise-of-stis-in-england-into-context/20203373.article?firstPass=false [Accessed 16 Nov. 2018].

Yeykelis, L., Cummings, J. and Reeves, B. (2014). *Multitasking on a Single Device: Arousal and the Frequency, Anticipation, and Prediction of Switching Between Media Content on a Computer*.

If you found this book interesting ...
why not read these next?

Doing Single Well

A Guide to Living, Loving and Dating without compromise

Doing Single Well will help you find fulfilment
in your single life, and if you want a partner,
to wait for one who is right for you.

Body Image Problems
& Body Dysmorphic Disorder

The Definitive Treatment and Recovery Approach

This unique and inspiring book provides simple yet highly effective self-help methods to help you overcome your body image concerns and Body Dysmorphic Disorder (BDD).

the Shaw mind
FOUNDATION

Creating hope for children,
adults and families

Sign up to our charity, The Shaw Mind Foundation

www.shawmindfoundation.org

and keep in touch with us; we would love to hear
from you.

*Our goal is to make help and support available for every
single person in society, from all walks of life.
We will never stop offering hope. These are our promises.*

TRIGGER™

The mental health & wellbeing publisher

www.triggerpublishing.com

Trigger is a publishing house devoted to opening conversations about mental health. We tell the stories of people who have suffered from mental illnesses and recovered, so that others may learn from them.

Adam Shaw is a worldwide mental health advocate and philanthropist. Now in recovery from mental health issues, he is committed to helping others suffering from debilitating mental health issues through the global charity he co-founded, The Shaw Mind Foundation. www.shawmindfoundation.org

Lauren Callaghan (CPsychol, PGDipClinPsych, PgCert, MA (hons), LLB (hons), BA), born and educated in New Zealand, is an innovative industry-leading psychologist based in London, United Kingdom. Lauren has worked with children and young people, and their families, in a number of clinical settings providing evidence based treatments for a range of illnesses, including anxiety and obsessional problems. She was a psychologist at the specialist national treatment centres for severe obsessional problems in the UK and is renowned as an expert in the field of mental health, recognised for diagnosing and successfully treating OCD and anxiety related illnesses in particular. In addition to appearing as a treating clinician in the critically acclaimed and BAFTA award-winning documentary *Bedlam*, Lauren is a frequent guest speaker on mental health conditions in the media and at academic conferences. Lauren also acts as a guest lecturer and honorary researcher at the Institute of Psychiatry Kings College, UCL.

Please visit the link below:
www.triggerpublishing.com

Join us and follow us...

@triggerpub
@Shaw_Mind

Search for us on Facebook